THE GREAT BRITISH SKRIPAL HOAX

Novichok in storyland

THE GREAT BRITISH SKRIPAL HOAX

By Nick Kollerstrom PhD

© 2019 N. Kollerstrom

ISBN   978-0-244-19256-3

Other books by the author:

Terror on the Tube, Behind the Veil of 7/7 – an Investigation 2012
How Britain Initiated both World Wars 2017
False flags over Europe – A Modern history of state-fabricated terror 2018
Who did 9/11? A view from across the Pond 2019

Contents

Novichok in storyland

Prelude: On Fictional History

Novichok, Skripal, Salisbury - We are now supposed to forget about all the loose ends of this story, as they fade away leaving only an unpleasant pain. Instead I here suggest that it is worth deconstructing this modern 'fairy tale from Hell'. The main victims of this tale are the two Russians, abducted by the British government, who we may never see again. But in addition the victims are *us, we the public*, as we are traumatised and impacted by the story, of what did *not* happen. We are also taught who to hate – why, the evil Russkies, of course.

There is indeed a profound and terrible evil in this story, but it is not beyond the Urals. The real, true enemies of mankind are, I suggest, Those Who Create Delusion and they are somewhat nearer home.

The British Intel deceptions and fabrications here reviewed have managed to harm *both* Trump *and* Putin. Why did the Democrats, in 2016, ask a British Intel agency to cook up their 'golden showers' dirty dossier on Trump, instead of doing it themselves? The sorrowful answer here has to be, that *British liars are the best.* British-Intel lies are somehow perceived as being more credible. This no doubt derives from a bygone era, when 'An Englishman's word is his bond' and the word of an Englishman was somehow reliable. If so, that capital is pretty well spent, one regrets to say.

Andrew Wood, a former British ambassador to Moscow, was employed by the Institute for Statecraft, and he passed on the Steele dossier to U.S. Senator John McCain, who gave it to FBI Director James Comey. The FBI used the dossier first to get federal warrants to spy on the Trump campaign, and, after Comey was fired, to launch a counter-intelligence investigation against Trump himself. Thereby an all-British pack of lies seems to have more or less paralysed the US government for the last two years.

The British Government now uses names like *Institute for Statecraft* and *Integrity Initiative* for blatantly warmongering anti-Russian mendacity. To quote Craig Murray here, "if the Integrity Initiative is promoting it, you know it is not true."[1] From producing fake dead duck pictures for the US president, to faking 'Novichok' samples from Porton down that are given to the Organization for the Prevention of Chemical Weapons – is there no limit?

Max Blumenthal ✓
@MaxBlumenthal

Replying to @MaxBlumenthal

The Integrity Initiative is just a small gear in a semi-covert military-intel & corporate backed op spanning Western govs, NGO's & media. This propaganda machine was built to hype a new Cold War, ramp up military spending & undermine any politician or critic who gets in the way.

♡ 433   10:00 PM - Dec 18, 2018

◯ 323 people are talking about this

The above tweet from US journalist Max Blumenthal describes about the shocking and secretive manner in which UK government funding has been misused, to promote hate and fear and nurture deep-state militarism. Ordinary folk

---

[1] Craig Murray, 'Ten Points I just can't Believe about the Official Skripal Story,' point no. 1, 7.3.19..

watching the news do not suspect that groups like these are involved in constructing and promoting the fake stories, such as the Skripal poisoning.

The good people of Salisbury might find that social togetherness could be experienced and developed if they were to collectively express their indignation and insist on a public enquiry into What Really Happened. The people of Salisbury have been traumatized and stressed as their home town was impacted by *fictional horror* - courtesy of their own Government. They need to start a campaign concerning 'Where is Yulia?' -'Release Yulia' - 'We demand to see Yulia,' etc. We ought surely to assume she is still alive - somewhere. May 11th as the date of Yulia's last 'appearance' would be a good anniversary date for this; as well as the 18th of May, when Sergei Skripal was said to have been discharged from Salisbury District Hospital, since when he has apparently vanished into thin air.

1

Novichok in Storyland

In the late autumn of 2017, a Sky-TV thriller series *Strike Back: Retribution* began, which wove a story of international intrigue involving an imaginary nerve poison called 'Novichok'. Thus, for example, Episode 4 featured: 'General Lázsló shuts down Section 20, forcing Donovan to work in secret. She discovers that Zaryn is in fact Karim Markov, a

Russian scientist who allegedly killed his colleagues with Novichok, a nerve agent they invented,' etc. In the film it was a 'binary' weapon, i.e. the toxin was made by mixing two compounds together. Let us consider these episodes:

Episode 4

November 21, 2017 (UK) and Feb. 23, 2018 (US)

Episode 5

November 28, 2017 (UK) and March 2, 2018 (US)

Episode 6

January   31, 2018 (UK) and March 9, 2018 (US)

The Empire has to tell us what it plans to do in advance, or so we're told: it's called 'Predictive programming.' As Webster Tarpley wrote in 2005: "No terrorist attack would be complete without the advance airing of a scenario docudrama to provide the population with a conceptual scheme to help them understand the coming events in the sense intended by the oligarchy" (*Synthetic Terror*, p.408). Supposedly, they obtain our tacit agreement by telling us in advance, or that's the theory.

Nina 🔁 Byzantina ✓
@NinaByzantina

It's strange that a British-American intelligence TV drama Strike Back had several episodes featuring Novichok nerve agent and Evil Russkies last year. Someone orchestrating political theater in the UK watches a lot of TV, or is advised by its producers.
en.wikipedia.org/wiki/Strike_Ba...

8:32 PM - Mar 15, 2018

(reference here is wiki/Strike_Back:_Retribution)

Whether or not the Skripal event was pre-planned, that ongoing TV series helped to create the script. It was a source of ideas, for those seeking an anti-Russian angle. Britain's Conservative government was greatly failing in its Brexit negotiations and needed some distraction, plus the British intervention in Syria was increasingly being exposed as *pro-terrorist,* whereby the deceptive 'White Helmets' were faking alleged Syrian government chemical attacks on the Syrian people.[2] British jets had been bombing Syrian cities for quite a long time, and why were they doing that? There was a perceived danger, that the Russian forces who had been invited into Syria by the legitimate government and who were fighting against ISIL or al-Qaeda, i.e. against the terrorists, would be perceived as the good guys. Some timely insertion of a counter-narrative was necessary.

Russia's chemical weapon stockpiles were finally destroyed in the autumn of 2017, and the Director-General of the OPCW stated[3]:

The completion of the verified destruction of Russia's chemical weapons programme is a major milestone in the achievement of the goals of the Chemical Weapons Convention. I congratulate Russia and I commend all of their experts who were involved for their professionalism and dedication. I also express my appreciation to the States Parties that assisted the

---

[2] See eg *Veterans Today*; 'Swedish Medical Associations Says White Helmets Murdered Kids for Fake Gas Attack Videos' 6.4.17 Gordon Duff (although NB The Swedish Doctors for Human rights did express some scruples about this VT account).

[3] opcw.org 27.9.17, 'OPCW Director-General Commends Major Milestone as Russia Completes Destruction of Chemical Weapons Stockpile under OPCW Verification.' See also SIPRI Yearbook for 2018, reporting on how Russia 'completed destruction of its stockpile in 2017' (p.348).

Russian Federation with its destruction program and thank the OPCW staff who verified the destruction.

Meanwhile, the British chemical weapons laboratory Porton Down had received over the last decade some seventy million dollars from the Pentagon for research and devlopment, for *further developing* nerve agents and other chemical weapons. They were tested on lab animals, with over a hundred thousand being 'used' for the Pentagon project. The effect of sulphur, mustard gas and also phosgene gas tests on the lungs of various animals was investigated. In this way the Pentagon gained access to Porton Down's scientific and technical capabilities, plus other test data. The US army regularly produces deadly viruses, bacteria and toxins in violation of the UN Convention on the Prohibition of Biological Weapons.[4]

So, while Russia was fully complying with destruction of its chemical weapons stockpiles, in a transparent and verifiable manner, the US and UK had been conducting such forbidden research, using live lab-animals.[5] That perspective may help us to appreciate the depth of mendacity involved in the Skripal story - which took place a mere few miles from the Porton Down laboratories.

For three weeks prior to the event the British army war-gamed 'Operation Toxic Dagger' on Salisbury plain

---

[4] 'The US Army regularly produces deadly viruses, bacteria and toxins in direct violation of the UN Convention on the prohibition of Biological Weapons:' *WMD America: Inside the Pentagon's Global Bioweapons Industry*, '21st Century Wire,' 21.1.18.
[5] 'Salisbury attack reveals $70 million Pentagon program at Porton Down' By Dilyana Gaytandzhieva 30.4.18

simulating a chemical warfare attack, over February-March 2018:

> The three-week exercise included company-level attacks and various CBRN (chemical, biological, radioactive and nuclear) scenarios based on the latest threats for ultimate realism, such as a raid on a suspected chemical weapons lab. It climaxes with a full-scale exercise involving government and industry scientists and more than 300 military personnel … casualty treatment was a key part of the Salisbury Plain exercise. A chemical decontamination area was set up not merely to treat 'polluted' commandos, but also any wounded prisoners they may have brought in; once cleansed, casualties can be treated in field/regular hospitals…[6]

State-fabricated terror normally features such a drill, that is conducted in synchrony with the event or just before it. The plans that mature during the drill, then *result in* the event.

2

The Trump 'Dirty Dossier'

As a double-agent Sergei Skripal had betrayed his Russian colleagues. He was jailed and then released on a

---

[6] Nuclear-news.net 'The Skripals and the unusual timing of chemical warfare exercises near Salisbury.' 6.4.18.

spy-swap. He had ostensibly been living quietly in Salisbury since then, but it seems that he had actually been helping with 'Orbis Business Intelligence' run by a shady ex-MI6 agent called Christopher Steele. The Democrat party in America had requested that he help them before the US election in brewing up dirt on Trump. They paid Steele to do this, assuming that Hilary Clinton would win and so such foul play would never see the light of day. But it did all emerge and the *New Yorker* called Steele 'the man behind the Trump dossier.'[7]

This 'dirty dossier' not only alleged Russian interference in US elections but also contained the so-called 'golden showers' document, weaving a story about Trump being in collusion with Putin if not a Russian agent. A "failed spy" had relied upon "made-up facts by sleazebag political operatives" as President Trump rightly observed.[8] As regards its influence, one must agree that:

> … the very dirty and obviously fake dossier on Donald Trump and Vladimir Putin has sustained the Russiagate scandal for almost two years in the United States, throwing this country into a McCarthyite hysteria..[9]

It formed 'the insane underpinning of the whole mad Mueller probe into "Russian collusion"'[10] (Robert Mueller was a former FBI Director). For two years the US

---

[7] New Yorker 12.3.18 'Steele the Man Behind the Trump dossier'
[8] Ibid.
[9] Larouchepac.com 'the British role in the Coup against the President is now exposed.' 10.1.19 See Appendix.
[10] Michael Anthony, 'The Alternative Skripal Narrative' on *The Saker* website, 17.2.19.

Department of Justice conducted an enquiry, into whether the US President was a Russian agent, where the *only evidence* for its treasonous claim was the Steele dossier. Even as late as February 2019 former FBI director Andrew McCabe was wondering on national TV if America's President is a Russian agent. Can a nation be governed under such circumstances? There is real evidence for interference in the 2016 US elections, however it was by the UK – not Russia.

In November of 2018 a UK 'Anonymous' collective started releasing tranches of documents about 'Integrity Initiative,' which derived from the 'Institute of Statecraft.' To quote again from the US Lyndon Larouche website, it comprised:

> … an international network of politicians, journalists, academics, foundations, and military officers engaged in a very dirty black propaganda campaign funded by the British Foreign and Commonwealth Office, NATO, Facebook, and such intelligence quangos as the Smith Richardson Foundation here in the United States, all while posing as a Scottish charity.

Funded by the UK government, it became swiftly apparent that its meaning was very much the opposite of integrity or statecraft: in a secret and mendacious manner it was generating anti-Russian propaganda. We may quote again from the US Larouche foundation (See Appendix), as to how British lies were being spread across Europe:

> This methodology, fully implemented in the British propaganda and regime change operation against Putin, which began with the Litvinenko poisoning in 2006 and dramatically escalated in 2014, has created

an astounding and deranged war fever against Putin in Britain and throughout Europe…

The Institute has recently opened major operations targeting Germany, seeking to smear and defame existing German networks urging peace with Russia while attempting to build the same war fever they have created in Washington and London.[11]

Key names appear in this shadowy organization: Christopher Steele, Mark Urban - the BBC political correspondent who started writing his book on the Skripal affair in 2017 a year *before* it had happened - and Pablo Miller OBE, a longtime 'handler' of Skripal. We may surmise that the latter moved to Salisbury after his release from Russia because Miller lived there. Miller was then working for Steele, his old boss at MI6, in the private intelligence firm *Orbi*s.

Names connected with the White Helmets in Syria also link to the the Institute of Statecraft. The White Helmets 'charity' claims to be rescuing kids from Syrian government attacks, whereas it has actually been concerned in a theatrical manner to fabricate mock chemical-weapons attack dramas. These ratify the US/UK city bombing of Syria, and also appear to have been involved in the harvesting of human organs and abduction of children.[12]

Sergei Skripal's help would have been needed in preparing the Steele dossier, to give an authentic-sounding Russian Intel angle. In the view of Craig Murray, the Dossier

[11] Ibid, ref. 7.
[12] Vanessa Beezley, 21st Century Wire, 24.2.19: 'WHITE HELMETS: Organ Traffickers, Child Kidnappers,Thieves, Terrorists, Propagandists… or 'Saints''?

had been written by a Russian "trained in the KGB tradition." After the whole thing backfired with Trump's unexpected electoral victory, followed by the publication of this 'dirty dossier,' it was gratifying to see those responsible in the hot seat.

Following this debacle, the notion of returning to his motherland could have assumed considerable urgency for Sergei Skripal. Would he not rapidly start to appear as a disposable asset? MI6 would surely assume that he would be discussing that option with his daughter as soon as she arrived: this being something they could not permit. He would not want to end up being 'Litvinenkoed.'

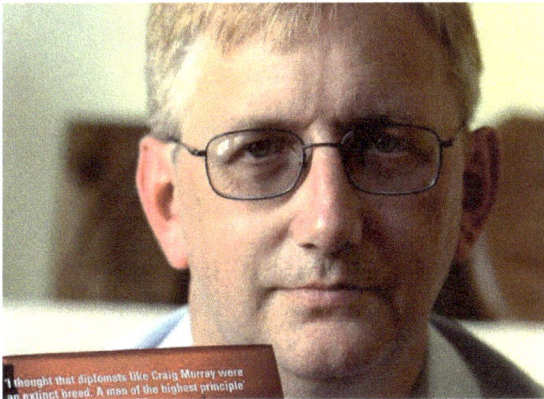

'I thought that diplomats like Craig Murray were an extinct breed. A man of the highest principle'

Craig Murray: a reliable source. His article 'Skripals – the Mystery Deepens' received three thousand comments.

3

Yulia pays a visit

On March 3rd, Yulia Skripal flew over to Salisbury from Moscow to visit her Father. Sergei Skripal's old friend Ross Cassidy, a construction worker, drove him over to Heathrow airport to pick her up. Mr Cassidy then noticed that Skripal seemed rather jumpy: 'Something had spooked Sergei in the weeks prior to the attack. He was twitchy, I don't know why, and he even changed his mobile phone.'[13] Mr Skripal had by no means fully retired from his life as a double-agent after his release from a Moscow jail in 2010; it is not hard to understand how he might be in such a state.

The day before, two Russians had flown over, visiting Salisbury, and then flew back around midnight on March 4th the day after. It seems that three seats were booked on that return flight, not two – one which was not used,[14] prompting speculation, as to whether Sergei Skripal was meant to return to Russia on that flight? There would have been every reason for him to wish to return, as he had living relatives over there. If he were then to tell what he knew, would that exert a dire effect upon the US-UK 'special relationship'? It would surely diffuse the war-propaganda that had been building up and enable Trump and Putin to talk to each other. But, for these very reasons, it could not be

---

[13] Ross Cassidy recalled this six months later in September as we'll see, but I'm suggesting it may be reliable.
[14] Disclosed in February 2019 by 'Bellingcat,' see M. Anthony 'The Skripal Case, an Alternative narrative' March 2019, off-Guardian.

allowed! Yulia had to put these options to him because no phone could be trusted.

The story given by the two Russians – as tourists visiting Salisbury cathedral – was not generally viewed as being very plausible, and the notion that they had come to deliver something seemed to make more sense. Their itinerary around Salisbury brought them within half a mile of the Skripals home: did they have a fake passport and air ticket which they somehow delivered to Mr Skripal? Arriving by train into Salisbury station at 11.48 am, they returned later that day: we'll see later on how the police obfuscated the return time, as if they had jumped on the 1.50 pm train returning to London.[15] Such a short visit would only make sense in terms of some sort of delivery.

On the morning of March 4th the father and daughter were (at first) said to have driven to the local cemetery where Mr Skripal's late wife and son were buried. Here is a possible timeline for events of that day:

* At 9:15am on 4 March Mr Skripal seen driving his car. They visit the Salisbury cemetery to pay respects to his dead wife.

* Two Russians allegedly arrive at Skripal door around 12-1 pm.

* Did Skripals return home around 1 pm & touch the doorknob?

* At 13:30 Mr Skripal's car was seen on the way towards the town centre.

* At 13:40 Sergei and Yulia go to Bishops Mill Pub in the

---

[15] Luke Harding, *The Guardian* 5.9.18 'Planes, trains and fake names: the trail left by Skripal suspects'

town centre.
* At 14:20 they dined at the Zizzi Restaurant.
* At 15:35 they left it.
* At 4.15 they are 'slumped' on a park bench.
* At 5.15 they are taken to Salisbury hospital.

This omits the duckpond scene which, if it happened, was after 1 pm.

The Zizzi restaurant, where the two had lunch

Thus, Mark Urban in his book tells how the couple walk from the Zizzi's restaurant towards the Maltings (where the park bench was) with some bread to feed the ducks, but then they have to sit down, they feel groggy, sweat profusely, et cetera.[16]

---

[16] M.Urban., *The Skripal Files*, p.213.

In contrast, we may turn to Rob Slane, a well-informed Salisbury local (whose website *the Blogmire* is possibly the best on the subject): he finds that 'there exists really clear footage of the couple feeding ducks next to the Avon playground' around 1.45 pm., which would be before lunch. He has also stated 'I have had it personally confirmed to me that they were in the pub between 15.00 and 15.30 – after lunch!' There are many CCTV cameras in The Mill pub, and as usual in such cases we're not shown any of it. Here is one local witness he cites:

> Sergei Skripal went for a drink with his daughter at 3pm at The Mill in Salisbury after eating at a Zizzi Italian restaurant. In the pub, they ordered two glasses of wine before Mr Skripal went to use the toilet. The witness, who did not want to be named, …[17]

It would seem that the authorities have wished to obfuscate the actual sequence, whereby after emerging from their house around or just after 1 pm, they drove off in their car, parked it in town, fed some ducks, went to have lunch in Zizzi's, went to have a drink at *The Mill*, and then strolled over through the shopping centre to The Maltings. This all sounds as if they were enjoying life and not as if they had both received a deadly poison. The picture shown of them in the pub together (see Chapter 11) looks cheerful enough.

---

[17] Theblogmire.com '10 main holes in the official narrative.' August 2018.

4

Food poisoning at Zizzi's?

Were the two poisoned while they had lunch at the Zizzi restaurant? That was the initial story, however, the image of Russian agents creeping into that elegant restaurant and surreptitiously adding a deadly poison to the food never made any sense, not least because no-one else in the restaurant was affected. The two had enjoyed a meal of risotto pesce with king prawns, mussels and squid rings in a tomato, chilli and white wine sauce. Subsequently the restaurant was closed down and staff uniforms worn on that day were burned (11th March). Even that theatrical act could not make the story appear credible.

A week later, around the 17th of March, police were murmuring that the Novichok had perhaps arrived in Yulia's suitcase, brought over from Moscow – implying that she herself had packed the poison, or at least knew it was there (*The Sun* 18 March 'Russian Plot'). Before that, the police had located it on the car door-handle, but neither of these stories seemed very credible. Finally the locus of the alleged deadly poison had to move again, and *three weeks after the event* it finally ended up located on the Skripal's home door handle (March 24th).

It was raining that day, and the 'gel' – if ever it had existed – would have been water-soluble.

Although the police claim to have CCTV records of Mr Skripal's car driving around Salisbury on that day, they have been strangely vague about whether the Skripals returned to their home at around noon, with different timelines being put out, retired and changed. Supposedly he must have shut his front door upon leaving, and thus became contaminated. Then he held his daughter's hand or arm thereby contaminating her, after which they drove around. They enjoyed lunch in a restaurant and a drink in a pub, then strolled down the central shopping arcade, coming into the park where a light drizzle was falling. The 66-year old man and his 33-year daughter collapsed simultaneously on a park bench, from a toxin received *three hours* earlier, remaining on that bench for an hour then being taken to hospital – with not a single photograph taken. Once again there are problems of credibility here.

Did the two of them suffer food poisoning from the restaurant, as argued by 'Moon of Alabama''s ('Bernhard') on the *Sputnik* RT program? That would indeed give us a pleasantly simple view of events:

> I believe that the Skripals suffered from simple food poisoning. They ate a Risotto Pesce with mussels at the Zizzi restaurant and unintentionally poisoned themselves with Saxitoxin, a natural 'nerve agent' that is also known as shellfish poison.

He went on to explain how British government officials then lifted the Novichok explanation from the *Strike Back* program:

> A day later the government woke up to that fact that the Skripal case could be used to divert from May's problems with the Brexit negotiations and

help in upcoming elections. They needed
something splashy, to blame it on Russia. Someone
in the Government's spin-master group came up
with 'Novichok'.[18]

On this view, what 'Moon of Alabama' calls 'the
Government's spin-master group' had to act quickly, and
were inspired by the *Strike-Back* TV series. Here is the BBC's
report, of how the couple were treated:

A doctor who was one of the first people at the
scene has described how she found Ms Skripal
slumped unconscious on a bench, vomiting and
fitting. She had also lost control of her bodily
functions. The woman, who asked not to be named,
told the BBC she moved Ms Skripal into the
recovery position and opened her airway, as others
tended to her father. She said she treated her for
almost 30 minutes, saying there was no sign of any
chemical agent on Ms Skripal's face or body. The
doctor said she had been worried she would be
affected by the nerve agent, but added that she
"feels fine". (8th March)

This 'high-security' couple in Salisbury, who would be being
closely monitored, are suddenly vomiting on a park bench.
The medic remained unaffected by any symptoms of nerve
poisoning.

Porton Down, Britain's main 'Bio-Hazard' research
centre, is located a mere six miles away from Salisbury town
centre. Immediately after the alleged collapse of the couple,

---

[18] 11.4.18 Sputniknews.com, 'How TV Spy Fiction Helped Sell the
Salisbury Poisoning'

we learnt that, 'The pair are currently in intensive care at Salisbury Hospital under supervision of experts from Public Health England's Centre for Radiation, Chemical and Environmental Hazards.' That was in The *Mirror* on March 6th. In other words, experts from Porton Down were looking after them, and why should that be? We the public were not told of any nerve-poison until the next day, the 7th of March. But experts from Porton Down were immediately present in the hospital, looking after the couple.

5

A Nurse passing by

The startling identity of the 'off-duty Nurse' who was the first to arrive at the park bench - she just happened to be passing by - emerged almost a year later: she was none other than 'Colonel Alison McCourt,' the army's most senior nurse! She and her daughter both 'treated' the Skripals for which her daughter received an award. She was skilled in dealing with chemical weapons injuries. She stated in a TV interview that 'the woman [Yulia Skripal] was not breathing at the time we found her,' which did not match her initial story. Alison McCourt must have known what was going on, and so the fact that she allowed her daughter to treat the couple indicates that no nerve agent was present.

The Skripals were taken to hospital, and then the next day's medical report had them treated for the drug Fentanyl. The *UK Clinical Services Journal* website reported that the couple were treated for Fentanyl poisoning in Salisbury hospital over the first day March 5th , although that statement was deleted some weeks later.[19] Fentanyl has a reputation as a 'date-rape' drug because it makes people feel sleepy and flop about, unlike a nerve-poison. As a synthetic 'opioid' it can be a recreational drug. Salisbury District Hospital declared a 'major incident' after 'two patients were exposed to an opioid.'

Dilyana Gaytandzhieva
@dgaytandzhieva

The #Skripals were allegedly exposed to the drug #Fentanyl, not the #Novichok nerve agent, according to information obtained from the UK Clinical Services Journal
clinicalservicesjournal.com/story/25262/re...
10:24 PM - Apr 26, 2018

Then on March 7th we heard about Detective Superintendent Nick Bailey, as being in hospital in a coma and 'fighting for his life.' The next day it was revealed that he had arrived at the park bench at around 4.30 pm, and 'caught' the nerve agent. Then after that on the 9th the story changed, and he had visited the Skripals house where he had been poisoned (Sir Ian Bair). Upon release from hospital, Nick Bailey said that his experience had been "completely surreal" and added, "normal life for me will probably never be the same" – doubtless the effect of a Fentanyl coma. He

---

[19] The article seems to have been up over 26-7th April, but then the Bulgarian journalist Dilyana Gaytandzhieva published this on her social media account, after which its text was changed from 'the drug Fentanyl' to 'a substance.' Presently the online *Clinical Services Journal* article of March 5th 'Response Unit Called As Salisbury Hospital Declares "Major Incident"' alludes merely to 'what is believed to be an opioid.'

then leaves the stage, so to speak, and we hear no more from him.

So two very senior people, one from the police and the other, the British Army, were just passing by and 'helped' the Skripals.

How did a Detective Superintendent come to be just walking by? How had he been poisoned when the nurse and her daughter who earlier treated the couple were OK? Clive Ponting, an old civil-service whistle-blower, reckoned that: 'the policeman who 'just happened' to be around was almost certainly the special branch "minder" who was keeping Yulia under surveillance.'[20] One could say much the same for the nurse, Colonel Alison McCourt.

Colonel Alison McCourt: just passing by?

---

[20] Craig Murray blog 28.4.19 'Probable Western Responsibility for Skripal poisoning'

6

A Premeditated Event?

Was the whole event premeditated? Mark Urban OBE, the Diplomatic and defence editor for the BBC, had been an officer in Britain's Royal Tank Regiment together with Pablo Miller – Sergei Skripal's handler. Mr Urban *had already been interviewing* Sergei Skripal for a book the previous year prior to the event, which seemed rather strange. When the story broke and he was the go-to spokesperson on the matter, no-one mentioned this! This curious fact only emerged in July of 2018, a few months before his book came out: people wondered how much he had been told by British intelligence on this matter. Had he for example discussed the Trump dossier in his meetings with Pablo Miller and Skripal? He never gave straight answers to these questions. But, when I heard him speak on LBC radio – as a main government spokesperson on the topic - he was articulate and very convincing.

alex thomson ✔
@alextomo

Follow ⌄

About the only decisive public move by the authorities has been to censor MSM via a D Notice last week from fully identifying Mr Skripal's MI6 handler living nearby...

9:14 am - 12 Mar 2018

The Government slapped not one but two D-notices upon any mention of Pablo Miller, within a week after the event.

He was Skripal's MI6 handler and they used to meet up at least once a month. As Craig Murray surmised, "That the government's very first act on the poisoning was to ban all media mention of Pablo Miller makes it extremely probable that this whole incident is related to the Trump dossier and that Skripal had worked on it."

Let us suppose that the double-agent Skripal wanted to return to Russia, because his mother and son had both died, buried in the Salisbury graveyard, whereas his grandmother was still alive in Russia as was his daughter Yulia. Russia might have accepted such a deal if there was a prospect of him spilling the beans about the alleged Russian interference in the US elections, cooked up by MI6.

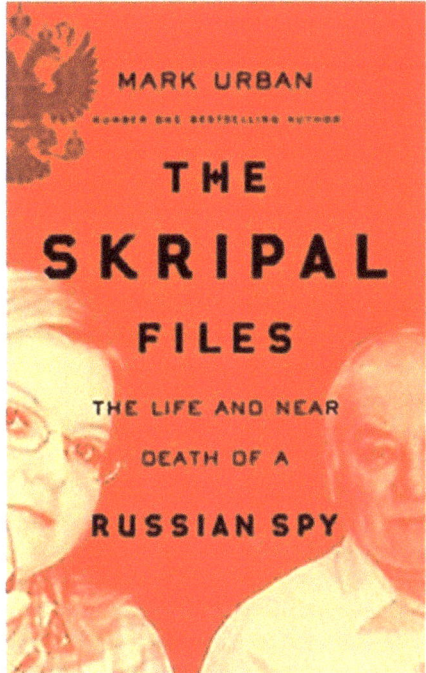

Both Skripals had their mobile phones switched off over four hours on that cold, Sunday morning[21] – or, were their phones only closed off to British intelligence? If such a plan existed, then MI6 would be suspecting and anticipating it –

---

[21] Craig Murray 6.9.18 'Skripals: The Mystery Deepens' (NB, this gained three thousand comments!)

after all, who can say when a double agent is going to turn again?

Sergei Skripal had seemed stressed, agitated and in a hurry to leave at the Zizzi's restaurant, as the staff there recalled. Could it be that he had an appointment at the park with someone, maybe with one of the two Russian visitors, or even with his handler Pablo Miller? MI6 may have been uneasy about his phone being blocked from them for several hours.

Clearly, someone would have had to give the drug to both of them *before* they collapsed on the park bench. Some witnesses have described the two as being catatonic and mmobile as if severely drugged, though I'm doubtful about these.[22] No-one has come up with any credible suggestion as to how such a drug could have been administered, to both of them. It is easier to imagine that some Fentanyl-like substance was administered to them in the ambulance on their way to the hospital.

Fentanyl was also reported in a local news site *Devon Live* on the next day, March 5th:

> It is understood that police suspect fentanyl, a synthetic opiate many times stronger than heroin, may have been involved. A man and a woman are in a critical condition and up to 10 other people are involved.
>
> Officers and paramedics were called to The Maltings shopping centre in Salisbury after the man and a woman fell ill. The woman, who was unconscious, was airlifted to Salisbury district

---

[22] e.g., Freya Church and <u>Destiny Reynolds</u>.

hospital at about 4.15pm, while the man was taken
by ambulance.

The 'Wiltshire Air Ambulance' did indeed land at 4.53 pm in
Sainsbury's car park, remaining there for ten minutes before
taking off - but we lack any account of who got in or out of
it. Again this could look like part of a pre-arranged narrative,
within the 'Operation Toxic Dagger.' The article had the
rather fictional title, 'Major chemical incident declared
after ten people vomited fentanyl and two are critically ill.'

Months later, Mr Skripal's friend Ross Cassidy, a haulage
contractor, recalled that the Skripals had been at home that
day until after 1 pm – as one might expect for a father and
daughter just reunited. [23] Ross Cassidy commented on the
location of their home:

> It would have been far too brazen for them [alluding
> to the two alleged perpetrators] to have walked down
> a dead end cul-de-sac in broad daylight on a Sunday
> lunchtime … Sergei's house faces up the cul-de-sac.
> He had a converted garage that he used as his office –
> this gives a full view of the street… Almost always,
> Sergei used to open the door to us before we had
> chance to knock.

From his office, Sergei could look down the little street and
see anyone coming: doubtless why MI6 chose that house for
him, when he moved to Salisbury.

Ross Cassidy tried to visit the Skripals in hospital, but
was denied access. Ditto for a team from *Russia Today*
television, they arrived at the Salisbury hospital but were
denied access to the Skripals. *Nobody* was allowed – no

---

[23] 9th September *Daily Mail*, 'Speaking for the first time.'

friends, no relatives. With headlines around the world and diplomats being expelled, it was strange to have no testimony. But, the BBC's correspondent Mark Urban gathered that Ross Cassidy was allowed to visit after Yulia had regained consciousness towards the end of March. She was discharged 9th of April.

Figure: Mr Ross Cassidy

Ian56 @Ian56789 · Mar 14

So this must be really serious!
Chemical Weapons experts in full Biological Warfare gear examine the bench in Salisbury Town Center where Sergei #Skripal was found.
Pedestrians look on without care from 10 yards away.

70   393   443

Figure: Removal of the park bench

27

7

Russia is Accused

Thirty senior cabinet ministers gathered together in Whitehall on the morning of Wednesday March 7th, maybe in the underground COBRA office,[24] and these included the Home Secretary Amber Rudd and Foreign Secretary Boris Johnson. On the previous day the word 'Novichok' had started to be used – and yet, noted Mark Urban of this group:

> None of them harboured any doubt that Russia was responsible for what had happened in Salisbury.[25]

If we assume he was correct - and he seems well-informed – we ought surely to enquire, as to the source of such an extraordinary collective certainty, given the complete, total absence of evidence pointing in any such direction.

Psychologists need to discuss how such collective certainty is achieved in the absence of any relevant evidence: could it be some spell, whereby the Reds-under-the-beds paranoia of the last century had somehow been reactivated?

On March 12th, a week after the event, Britain's Prime Minister Theresa May first hurled the dreadful accusation at Russia: a 'military-grade nerve agent of a type developed by Russia' had been used. Craig Murray commented:

---

[24] Cabinet Office Briefing Room A.
[25] *The Skripal Files*, p.234.

> The "novichok" group of nerve agents will almost certainly have been analysed and reproduced by Porton Down. That is entirely what Porton Down is there for [and] Porton Down has acknowledged in publications it has never seen any Russian "novichoks"… The UK government has absolutely no "fingerprint" information such as impurities that can safely attribute this substance to Russia…. There has in fact never been any evidence that any "novichok" ever existed in Russia itself.[26]

What was this deadly agent, more or less hitherto unknown, which the media were assuring us was more deadly than strychnine? Chemical-weapons experts were seen looking for it, in full protective gear. It was not on any official list of banned nerve agents – as Dr Trapp, a former Secretary of OPCW, declared:

> OPCW does not hold any information on Novichok … Novichoks have indeed not been declared as part of a CW stockpile or past CW production programme by any state party.[27]

Or as Nafeez Ahmed wrote on his blog, 'both Porton Down's Dr. Black and the OPCW's Science Advisory Board fundamentally questioned the "existence" of Novichok'.

The UK refused to comply with Russia's request for a sample of the alleged "novichok" and blocked their resolution at the UN calling for a "co-operative international investigation in line with OPCW standards" (15th March). Was not the UN set up for this very purpose, viz. resolving

---

[26] 13th March, 'Russian to Judgement'
[27] 27 March, Nafeez Ahmed blog.

international tensions by informed debate? All through this brazenly fabricated tale, we find a *complete absence of supporting evidence*: as if the mere word of the UK government should be enough, for the media and UK allies to accept their ever-changing tale.

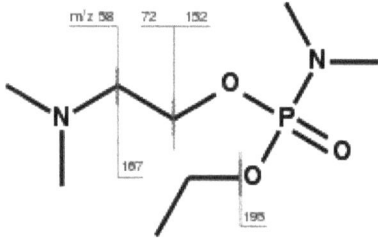

Theresa May did not allow the OPCW to become involved in the Salisbury event, until a couple of weeks had gone by – by which time anything could have been done to the samples. The director-general of OPCW Jose Bustani wondered, 'Why didn't they call immediately the OPCW? … They could have done this beforehand, before accusing Russia directly.'[28] But, there was a hidden agenda and the secret plotting of British Intel could never have survived proper scrutiny by experts in such a manner.

With restrained irony, a *Russia Today* program commented on 'curious parallels between the plots in *Homeland* and *Strike Back* and the media coverage of the Skripal poisoning drama:'[29]

---

[28] RT 7.4.18 'You can't decide in 24 hours.'
[29] Sputniknews.com 11 April 'How TV Spy Fiction Helped Sell the Salisbury Poisoning'

UK locates source of Salisbury nerve agent

Security services believe they have pinpointed the location of the covert Russian laboratory that manufactured the weapons-grade nerve agent used in Salisbury....

thetimes.co.uk

Apr 05, 2018

<u>Figure:</u> A witty image appeared in *The Times* on April 5th, entitled 'UK locates source of Salisbury nerve agent.' Even a British journalist, it would appear can experience a desire to tell the truth.

In the opening episode a government traitor is assassinated, poisoned with a nerve agent. While it is initially unclear who the culprits are, in episodes that broadcast on March 4 (the day the Skripals were found) and March 11 make it clear that a Russian intelligence 'active measures' unit were behind the poisoning.

A later episode had an FBI agent, Dante Allen, turned by Russian intelligence, then unmasked by our hero Carrie Mathison, who then poisons him with a nerve agent to trick him into thinking he is going to die, and to make him confess! The next episode broadcast on April 8 showed Dante recovering in hospital, with the Russian assassin demanding that his superiors let him assault the hospital to get to the agent.

On the same day the British media were reporting that the Skripals, who were still in hospital, were so terrified of rabid Russian assassins that they were going to be given new lives and new identities in America. Here one can only quote the Moon of Alabama: "Isn't it astonishing how 'life' follows the course of last week's TV drama?[30]

The OPCW were supposedly given a sample of the fabled Novichok wiped off from the door-handle. They commented that the sample was 'of high purity' which was probably their way of saying that they reckoned it had come straight from Porton Down[31] - which it probably had.

---

[30] www.moonofalabama.org 'The British Governments 'Novichok drama' was written by whom?'
[31] Craig Murray, 'Ten Points' (ref 1) 7.3.19.

Turning the pages of Mark Urban's authoritative book on the Skripal saga, we eagerly wait to hear how he and the entire British establishment reached their conclusion of Russian guilt. But all he says is, that

> if it [the UK] had specific intelligence about how the Skripal operation was mounted, the UK was not releasing it...'

We also gather that the director of Porton Down told sky news that 'his labs had not been able to trace the Salisbury Novichok samples to Russia,'[32] on April 3rd. I challenge any reader to peruse Mark Urban's book and find a single scrap of evidence for the accusation, that 'Russia did it:' all we get, is hearsay and innuendo.

8

Letter from an honest man

In the first week after the event, media stories averred that dozens of Salisbury residents had been affected by this nerve agent. But, the scary headlines ended after a carefully-worded letter appeared in *The Times,* from a senior medic at Salisbury general hospital, on 16th of March:

> Sir,
>
> Further to your report ("Poison exposure leaves almost 40 needing treatment", March 14), may I

---

[32] *The Skripal files*, pp. 252, 261.

clarify that no patients have experienced symptoms of nerve gas poisoning in Salisbury and there have only been three patients with significant poisoning. Several people have attended the emergency department concerned that they may have been exposed. None has had symptoms of poisoning and none has needed treatment. Any blood test performed have shown no abnormality. No member of the public has been contaminated by the agent involved.

Stephen Davies

After that straightforward testimony from a local medic, the stories evaporated, they vanished like a dream – they just had not happened!

Somewhat in response to this letter, Britain's 'Off-Guardian' reached its position of radical scepticism. Referring to Novichok as 'still largely mythical,' it advised:

Extreme scepticism is required here. An undisclosed agenda is driving things and driving them so hard even members of the political establishment are concerned... almost immediately upon this incident occurring a media campaign of almost unprecedented intensity began to generate what looked like a pre-prepared story that the Skripals had been poisoned by Russia. This claim has been "supported" by untruths and manipulations so questionable even anonymous FCO [Foreign and Commonwealth Office] sources are worried... The government and media are lying, leaping to conclusions and propagandising. Their claims about novichoks are unsubstantiated and seem to fly in the face of all published research. The media are trying to work up a jingoistic anti-Russia hysteria that has no parallel in recent times. Not even the 2003 media frenzy to get public opinion behind the illegal war on Iraq reached these heights.   (16 March: 'UK's "Novichok" program exposed as lies')

Discerning British citizens have had two reliable sources to consult over the whole affair: the *Off-Guardian* and the blog of ex-British diplomat Craig Murray. *That's about all,* and these sources have so to speak rescued our sanity amidst the maelstrom of lies from HM Government.

But, the story of local poisonings refused to die and a 'duckpond' tale surfaced a week later: the Skripals standing by their local duckpond had given bread to some youngsters to feed the ducks. The lads had become ill, and The Sun told its readers how a 12-year old lad was 'too scared to go out now' after the 'terrifying attack.' (28.3.18). A year later (18 April 2019) the *New York Times* revealed how this narrative had been used as a basis for Trump expelling sixty Russian diplomats. Then, local experts denied the story: "No children or animals were harmed in the Novichok attack in Wiltshire last year, health officials have said."33 It is said that the duck-feeding occurred around 1.15 ie right after they left home and before they reached the Zizzi restaurant (or the pub - it remains unclear which of these was first). The point here is that if Sergei really had been contaminated by Novichok, then the youngsters would have been

---

[33] The Guardian, 18 April, 'No children or ducks harmed by novichok, say health officials'

contaminated. If the roof of their house has been removed and if the Zizzi restaurant had been closed down and deconstructed, then how come the duckpond contamination did not take place?

That duckpond story re-surfaced a year later, as we'll see in Chapter 15, when the President of the United States was moved by the tale. It is surely appropriate that the newspapers should then publish a picture of the wrong duckpond, the one in the prestigious Queen Elizabeth Gardens - nowhere near where the Skripals are supposed to have been on that day: *O what a tangled web we weave…*

9

Brave Jeremy Corbyn response

'We don't do fantasy politics' was the initial response from the French government's spokesperson, after Theresa May announced that the Russian diplomats were to be expelled, adding that it would need 'firm proof' of Russian

involvement before it gave support. But alas this commendable *sang froid* did not last long, and a mere one day later on March 15th without any additional evidence coming to light, France joined in with the US, UK and Germany in blaming Russia for the alleged poisoning of the two Skripals.

Likewise, the British opposition leader Jeremy Corbyn cautiously warned against taking steps against Russia without first presenting evidence, and he ventured to call the intelligence on the matter 'problematic.' (March 14th) At once he found himself being assaulted in a vicious propaganda campaign: a BBC discussion of the Skripal affair was against a background of him photoshopped into Red Square and wearing a Russian hat. A tweet from 'Integrity Initiative' damned him as a 'useful idiot' working for the Kremlin. This was merely on account of his hesitation in accepting the Government's narrative, and sensibly requesting that the House needed to be given some evidence linking Russia to the Novichok story.

One is shocked that Government-funded anonymous persons can get away with such defamatory accusation. The venom here emanating from such sources as 'Integrity Initiative,' against people who were doubting the Government's narrative, had the purpose of preventing rational discussion of the Skripal affair, ensuring that a pre-ordained blame-Russia response prevailed. The hate-and-fear thereby generated enables the mainstream consensus to pass unchallenged: a 'Phantom Menace' *which does not actually exist* is mocked up, where the evil behavior attributed to it has actually come from some echelon of our own Government, or some military arm thereof. Thereby dissenting voices can be smeared as somehow collaborating with it.

Jeremy Corbyn's sickening support of Soviet empire
I remember the StB clearly. The Státní Bezpecnost, or State Security, was a pervasive part of my life in Communist-era Czechoslovakia. As the lone...
thetimes.co.uk

Integrity Initiative
@InitIntegrity

Follow

"Mr Corbyn was a "useful idiot", in the phrase apocryphally attributed to Lenin. His open, visceral anti-westernism helped the Kremlin cause, as surely as if he had been secretly peddling Westminster tittle-tattle for money..."

4:19 AM · 23 Feb 2018

Figures: anti-Corbyn tweets from *Integrity Initiative*

On March 14ᵗʰ, a couple of days after Theresa May's accusation against Russia, Corbyn found himself being denounced in the Commons because of a rather sensible comparison he was making, between the Skripal allegation and the UK Government's 'Dodgy dossier' of some years earlier, which had started the Iraq war. He further asked, should not the OPCW have first been consulted? Many in his own Labour party were angrily denouncing him, as if Russian guilt had been established.

But too soon, alas, Corbyn folded and endorsed the Government's view, going even beyond it and affirming: "the nerve agent used has been identified as of original Russian manufacture." Even Theresa May had not said that! Her weasel words had only been, that it was 'of a type developed by Russia.'

10

Russian Diplomats Expelled

Three weeks after the event, May announced "the largest collective expulsion of Russian intelligence officers in history" and NATO nations were happy to follow suite. One hundred and fifty were expelled, followed by tit-for-tat Russian expulsions so that some *three hundred* diplomats were expelled. After the cooked-up WMD dossier produced by British Intel in 2003, which got the Iraq war going, were international diplomats *again* prepared to take the word of a British government?

What possible motive could the Russians have for doing such a thing? In June Russia was hosting the World Cup, and a scandal like this was the very last thing it needed. Skripal had been released to live in Salisbury as a result of a spy-swap, and it was the established ethic of such deals that spies thus released had to be left alone afterwards.

A Chinese view is here of interest (*Global Times*, 27 March):

> The British government did not provide evidence that linked Russia to the crime but was confident from the beginning there could be no other "reasonable explanation" for the attempted assassination…. The fact that major Western powers can gang up and "sentence" a foreign country without following the same procedures other countries abide by and according to the basic tenets of international law is chilling. …
>
> It is beyond outrageous how the US and Europe have treated Russia. Their actions represent a frivolity and recklessness that has grown to characterize Western hegemony that only knows how to contaminate international relations.

Too right! It seemed that Britain no longer had diplomats, and that international diplomacy had been replaced by insults and name-calling by boorish UK officials - who would merely smirk at Russian appeals to due process and international conventions.

On whose word could one rely? Many turned to former British diplomat Craig Murray for guidance and 'Thedeepstate.com' wondered in this context, "Is former

British Ambassador Craig Murray the only knowledgeable and honest person the UK government can produce? It certainly seems that way." Murray's view was that 'If they exist at all, Novichoks were allegedly designed to be able to be made at bench level in any commercial chemical facility' and he quoted the ex-Soviet scientist Mizayanov: "One should be mindful that the chemical components or precursors of A-232 or its binary version novichok-5 are ordinary organophosphates that can be made at commercial chemical companies."[34]

Insofar as they exist, these would be a fairly unremarkable group of organic compounds. Murray has called out Boris Johnson, then Britain's Foreign Secretary, as being an outright liar on this matter.[35] In retrospect, everything stated by Craig Murray on this topic has so far turned out to be correct... and that is a reputation worth having.

A few days before the expulsion of Russian diplomats, a court judgement published a sworn statement by Porton Down from their analysis:

> Porton Down Chemical and Biological Analyst blood samples from Sergei Skripal and Yulia Skripal were analysed and the findings indicated exposure to a nerve agent or related compound. The samples tested positive for the presence of a

---

[34] 14th March, Craig Murray 'The Novichok Story Is Indeed Another Iraqi WMD Scam.' In the earlier-mentioned TV thriller program, one heard of this 'binary' weapon concept, whereby two harmless substances are mixed together to produce the nerve poison.

[35] Craig Murray, 22 March: 'Boris Johnson A Categorical liar.'

Novichok class nerve agent or closely related agent.

– from which Craig Murray concluded,

> This sworn Court evidence direct from Porton Down is utterly incompatible with what Boris Johnson has been saying. The truth is that Porton Down have not even positively identified this as a "Novichok", as opposed to "a closely related agent". Even if it were a "Novichok" that would not prove manufacture in Russia, and a "closely related agent" could be manufactured by literally scores of state and non-state actors.

> This constitutes irrefutable evidence that the government have been straight out lying – to Parliament, to the EU, to NATO, to the United Nations, and above all to the people – about their degree of certainty of the origin of the attack.[36]

Initially, one gathered, Trump was reluctant to expel the Russian diplomats. But then, the CIA's director (on or around the 23rd of March) showed him some moving photographs of young children in hospital, who had been poisoned by the Salisbury attack, plus some pictures of dead ducks likewise caused by the deadly Novichok. The heart of the US President was moved by these fake stories, and he went along with what the CIA director told him was the 'strong option,' of expelling sixty Russian diplomats.[37] One might have supposed that, after two years of his presidency

---

[36] Craig Murray, 'Boris Johnson a categorical liar' 22 March (site now blocked).
[37] *The Guardian* 16.4.19 'Novichok poisonings.' Craig Murray, 16.4.19 'The Official Skripal Story is a Dead Duck.'

had been ruined by a total pack of lies coming from this very same UK 'intelligence' group, he would be capable of some degree of scepticism, but … no.

11

A Lovely New Yulia

Let's come back to that last afternoon, when the Skripals enjoyed a drink together. One can discern the photographer reflected in the mirror behind them. Media sources later obscured this 'man in the mirror' image, after the D-notices banning any allusion to Pablo Miller had appeared; which would tend to suggest that the image was taken on that day by Pablo Miller. A couple of other images of father and daughter have been released, enjoying a drink together. We

© Not known

note Yulia's face, which is plump and round, with hair parted on the left.

<u>Figure</u>: the old, pre-Novichok Yulia

A month later, on April 5th a phone call from Yulia to her cousin Viktoria in Russia came out with the news that the couple were OK and recovering and that she hoped to return to Russia! While still in hospital, did she borrow somebody's mobile phone and call her cousin in Moscow?[38] 'I woke up over a week ago' she said - implying that they had been in a coma for several weeks:

> Later, let's talk later. In short, everything is OK ... Everything's OK. He's resting now, he's sleeping [i.e.,

<u>Figure</u>: the new, improved Yulia

---

[38] For text see: Mark.Urban, *The Skripal files*, pp.266-7.

Figure: the new, improved Yulia

her father]. *Everyone's health is OK. No one has had any irreversible [harm]. I'm being discharged soon.*

Viktoria can be heard telling her cousin *"If I get my visa tomorrow, on Monday I will fly to you"* and Yulia responds, *"nobody will give you a visa."* One sensed that this call was rather believable. Sure enough, the British government did refuse to grant a visa to Viktoria: why would it not want Yulia's closest relative to come and console her, at this most stressful moment in her life??

After all the government stories of how deadly the stuff was plus the accusation of murder made against Russia with all of NATO expelling its diplomats – suddenly, everything's fine!

It was then reported on 8th April as if in response to this unplanned phone call that the couple were going to be shipped over to the US with changed identities.

Six weeks after her release from the Salisbury hospital on April 11th, Yulia made her one and only media appearance on 23rd May. A new, slimline Yulia appeared and the world marvelled at the change. She no longer needed glasses and had lost so much weight in hospital. Her hair, much thicker, was now *parted on the right*. It rustled as she moved her head – had she been having some beauty treatment? The story went viral[39].

This charming Yulia here appears as improved and younger-looking after the Novichok attack. Gone is the old, frumpy Yulia as the marvellous Novichok elixir wiped years off her appearance! Verily, British intelligence is a Hall of Mirrors.

There was a prominent scar on her thorax, and questioned about that she only remarked that her treatment had been "invasive, painful and depressing."[40] In her carefully scripted appearance, we see her wandering out of a wood along a winding path, no doubt expressing the magical 'renewal' process. She then sat down and read out a statement, concerning which a Russian embassy spokesman commented:

> The video shown only strengthens our concerns as to the conditions in which she is being held. Obviously, Yulia was reading a pre-written text. More than that, judging from quite a few elements,

---

[39] Some months later an unlikely tale about Novichok in a perfume-bottle appeared – inspired by this witty image?

[40] The Salisbury doctors told the BBC that 'the Skripals were heavily sedated, to receive artificial ventilation and to protect them from brain damage': bbc.co.uk 29th May, 'How the Skripals were saved.'

the text was a translation from English and had initially been written by an English-speaker.[41]

Others pointed out that her text *did not blame* Russia – had she maybe insisted on that point? On March 21st a Russian source complained, 'Moscow is surprised that UK authorities deny consular access to Skripal's daughter in violation of international norms.'[42] None of her neighbours, friends or relatives had been allowed to see her, not in hospital or anywhere else since March 4th. Not even Ross Cassidy was allowed to see them, and a Russian TV crew which tried to get into Salisbury hospital was thwarted.

The 89-year old mother of Sergei and Yulia's grandmother Yelena – who is being cared for by Viktoria – received a phone call, on her 90th birthday:

> She [Julia} called and was actually with Sergei. She told me: "I'm with daddy he is beside me but he can't speak as he has a pain in his throat"... He can't speak because he's got a tracheostomy, that pipe, which will be taken off in three days. Now when he speaks with that pipe, his voice is first of all very weak and secondly, he makes quite a lot of wheeze. He had been in some pain (24th July).

In this conversation, Yulia strangely kept saying to her grandmother, 'Everything is fine, everything is perfect' in a

---

[41] Mirror, 23 May 'Yulia Skripal appears for first time since Novichok'

[42] The Salisbury National Health Service Foundation Trust sought leave in a three-day secret hearing of the Court of Protection (20-22 March) to take blood samples from the 'Skripals' – from which we gather, that even while they were staying in a public hospital, the NHS was unable to obtain blood samples ('the Williams Judgement').

Figure: this joke 'new, improved Yulia' image went viral. Note its 'perfume bottle,' months before the UK police claimed to have found it!

way that some found suspicious. She made no effort to convey a message from Sergei to his mother, which led some to suspect that he was not there.[43] *If* what she said was true, that her father was still having the tracheostomy operation, they would have to have been in the hospital. That would be strange, four months after the event, and two months after we were told he had been released from hospital. Nor does the message well accord with her earlier phone call to Viktoria when she had said that her father was fine.

Months later in October, Viktoria confirmed that there had been direct contacts with her cousin Yulia, who planned to return to Russia once her father was better.

Eleven months later, we learnt that the Novichok is still so deadly, that the whole roof of the Skripal's home needs replacing, by yellow-clad security agents wearing so military bio-hazard suits etc. First the doorknob, then roof timbers?

I have given a couple of talks on the subject of this booklet. I showed all of the Yulia pictures to the audiences and asked their opinion. By a show of hands, a huge majority reckoned that they were two different women, pre- and post- Novichok.

12

Death of a Drug-addict

The Skripal's cat had to be put down and by mid-April it appeared as being the only really dead thing in the whole

---

[43] *Russia Insider* article by Rob Slane, 'Where is Sergei Skripal?'

story: or we should say, officially dead, as some were surmising it had merely been taken to Yulia, wherever she was.

Figure: 'only a cat has died?'

The story was threatening to become humorous, with discussions about the house cat-flap. Two hundred diplomats expelled by NATO nations around the world, massive sanctions against Russia being prepared, and only a cat has died? In mid-March at the United Nations, the UK justified the expulsion_of two dozen Russian diplomats by describing the nerve agent as "a weapon so horrific it is banned from use in war." Then Yulia declared they were both fine ... It became evident that, in order to restore *gravitas* to the British story, a real death was needed.

How could that be arranged, four months after the event? A homeless drug-addict staying in a hostel in Salisbury called Dawn Sturgess who had a partner Charlie Rowley housed at a hostel in Muggleton Road, Amesbury. One night she "was on the floor having a fit and foaming at the mouth" and soon Charlie Rowley was experiencing similar symptoms. The police at first assumed that they were ill due to a contaminated batch of drugs, or maybe overdosing on heroin or crack cocaine. Or, could the protean 'Novichok' have done this? It was reported that this 44-year old woman had died of a heart attack, and could that (numerically) follow on from poisoning of the 66-year old Sergei and 33-

year old Julia? An inquest into her death was opened but then adjourned. Some were unkind enough to doubt whether she had really died, after all there was no media coverage of her funeral, only a single video clip of a hearse carrying a coffin entering a "compound," with no onlookers or family members present.

A friend described Ms Sturgess as being a homeless alcoholic who suffered from post-natal depression after her son Aidan was born, who had been smoking weed and over the course of time had turned to harder drugs - she had become 'like a zombie.'[44] Her partner Mr Rowley was in the habit of going 'bin diving' where he would 'pick up fag butts, go into charity shop bins,' etc. One day while he was

[44] Holly Christodoulou *The Sun* 22.11.18 'Poison Death: Who was Dawn Sturgess'?

out rummaging in bins in the historic Queen Elizabeth Gardens in Salisbury, he picked up a perfume bottle that had been there for several months. It was 'boxed and sealed' in a cellophane wrapper, or so he told *the Guardian*. Because it was 'sealed, boxed and looked expensive' (25th July) he picked it up: "It was an oily substance and I smelled it and it didn't smell of perfume." (24th July) Despite this he gave it to his partner as a present – a fatal mistake.

This daft story left a cluster of unanswered questions a-hovering in the public mind: how did a sticky gel turn into a vapour that could be squirted from a bottle? How come park wardens didn't empty the bin for three months? Why would two Russian agents want to stroll through a park that was not on their way to or from wherever they were going, e.g. the train station, and casually toss the deadly poison away? How come whatever they had used magically ended up, boxed up and unopened like a present? Clearly the perfume bottle did not have their fingerprints on it, or the police would have pressed charges – which they haven't. Was there ever a coroner's report, declaring that death was by Novichok and not just heart failure? No, in fact, that did not appear. Then last but not least, who has got the bottle, if perchance it exists?

It was in the wake of this 'real death' that the US announced their Russian sanctions based upon the Novichok scam, in August (in fact on 8.8.18). A Russian embassy spokesman then stated, 'We have grown accustomed to not hearing any facts or evidence.' The rouble sank to its lowest level for nearly two years. Sagely commented one blogger, *"It looks like the "Novichok" British MI6 Hysteria is being uncorked again, in order to bring more US sanctions against Russia."* ('Hamlet Quest' on *Russian Insider* 8.8.18)

Under British law, where there is a suspicious death, a Coroner's Court hearing must be held, and this clearly applied to the death of Dawn Sturgess. There seemed to be a problem however, with the first such hearing held on 19 July 2018 being immediately adjourned, and then another inquest into her death in January 2019 also being postponed. They still could not reach a verdict, the Wiltshire coroner explained, despite having received advice from police, military, intelligence and toxicology experts. They evidently could reach no conclusion over her death and certainly no-one was prepared to comment upon what the alleged perfume bottle contained! Then in October 2019 the Coroner's Court issued a statement announcing that the inquest into her death had been adjourned indefinitely. This should have been a scandal, because it meant that the whole public narrative of her death had collapsed: none of the allegations made over the previous 18 months could be sustained. Presumably we should now return to the original, default position, of a drug-addict taking an overdose.

13

Damaged Memory

Charlie Rowley today (2019) is in a terrible state and his brother reckons he may not live much longer. His sight and balance are compromised and it's hard for him to sleep at night. He still cannot well remember what happened, but a year after the event he expressed the view that the British authorities 'have not been transparent' about what happened to Dawn Sturgess. He added, 'I feel like we're being kept in the dark about what really happened,' which is true enough. He claims to remember that the bottle he picked up was 'sealed with hard plastic' and needed a kitchen knife to open it. He therefore concluded, quite logically, that

It can't possibly be the same bottle that was used by the Skripals.[45]

He denies having found it in a park. When asked in a TV interview[46] "You're pretty sure when you were in the park on Friday afternoon that you didn't find [the bottle] there?" he replied, "I'm pretty sure. No I'm 100% sure, it wasn't in the park." That 'Friday' alluded to was June 29th, when the couple were visiting Salisbury – that being the day before the two fell synchronously into a coma at his home. In a subsequent ITV interview, where he was filmed being taken around Salisbury, he again expressed confidence that he had not found it in the park.

Though unsure where the bottle had come from, he remained certain that he had *not* found it in the park. While he lay unconscious for over a week, in the same Salisbury hospital as had treated the Skripals, the press speculated as to where the poison had come from. During that time Dawn passed away, ie she never regained consciousness. On the same day that he woke up, police reported having found a bottle: *in his house*, in Amesbury.

---

[45] *The Guardian*, 21.6.19
[46] ITV interview of 24th July, The Blogmire

That was on the 11th of July. Earlier, on the 5th we had been informed that the couple were critically ill in hospital, and that the poison had been 'identified' as the same Novichok that had poisoned Skripals. There had been, the *Evening Standard* assured us on that evening, a 'multi-million pound clean up' after the Skripals, with a hundred counter-terror agents working with Wiltshire police to try and detect, whatever it was that had poisoned the couple.

On the 6th the *Mirror* said that Charlie had found 'the container' in some bushes in the park, then a couple of days later it said that he had found 'a stash of vials or syringes' while 'scavenging' through bushes. But, those didn't last long: on the 13th we were told that 'a bottle had been found' at Charlie's home, which had tested positive for Novichok and that this had been found on the 11th. That was the first definite police statement about the container. If the police had been conducting an immense, multi-million pound search, how come it took them eleven days to spot a 'bottle' in Charlie Rowley's home, presumably left where the ill-fated couple had passed out?

Charlie awoke shortly after Dawn died, but with a fuzzy memory.

Charlie's brother endorsed the bush-in-the-park story, and he introduced the perfume bottle motif: the couple had 'picked up a perfume bottle in a park containing the nerve agent and sprayed it on themselves.' (The *Mail*, July 17th) This soon became the accepted narrative even though Charlie himself did not endorse it. He first comments on the 19th, when he averred that Dawn had sprayed the Novichok on her wrists 'from a discarded perfume bottle she came across on a day out,' then later on he would recall that it was found in a charity shop bin.

On the 24th of July, he gave his shocking account of how well wrapped up in a package the perfume bottle was, so that it was an *unused bottle*. The official story died on that day: can anyone maintain that covert Russian agents first poisoned the two Skripals synchronously then left another, separate bottle of the same deadly poison in a litter bin somewhere else, and if so why would they have wanted to do that? That litter bin had to remain miraculously unemptied for four months, while all the police and detectives were supposedly scouring the area fail to find any clues? We have been given a gradually-unfolding and changing story, none of which made any sense, with a real death *but* no inquest verdict, and one damaged human being remaining who can't quite remember what happened. The bottle itself may only have existed in Storyland.

14

Two Russian 'Tourists'

In September, the British police averred that two Russians Alexander Petrov and Russlan Boshirov were the guilty culprits. Why had it taken them six months to ascertain this? The two Russians had visited Salisbury on the 3rd and 4th of March. From the time of their arrival in Salisbury on that day they could have arrived at the house a little after noon – if that was in fact where they were going.

Had they done this, they surely would have had to be sure that Mr Skripal was not at home: they could hardly take the risk of him being in his office which faced up the cul-de-sac road, where he could see any visitors coming.

To place the toxin on the doorknob the two would have needed serious protective clothing, otherwise they would have been poisoned (see photos of the green outfits worn by the police). The police never provided evidence for anything resembling this. It is clear that no such event ever took place.

The BBC correspondent Karen Gardner recalled how, a couple of days after the incident, police officers had been mingling around the Skripals' front door -

> When I was here a year ago, I watched Wiltshire police officers with no or minimal protective clothing going in and out that front door. They were carrying coffee flasks. They appeared to have had refreshments in the house overnight. That was two days after the Skripals had collapsed, at the point the Met had taken over the investigation. Shouldn't those officers have been better protected?[47]

This conclusively refutes the official story.

The two Russians had flown over from Moscow on Friday, 2nd March and returned on Sunday the 4th. Six months later, the police alleged that the hotel room the two had stayed in was contaminated with Novichok[48] - the only scrap of evidence ever produced for this accusation. But why

---

[47] BBC Radio Wiltshire, 6th March.

[48] 6th September dailymail.co.uk 'Owner of hotel where novichok spies stayed for two nights was only told by police about his killer guests YESTERDAY.'

had they taken so long to reveal this? The owner of the hotel was taken aback by the news, protesting that he had known nothing about it until 4th September when the story broke! He 'had not been told' which rooms they stayed in, of a room in his hotel allegedly contaminated with Novichok! Why, wondered Viktoria Skripal, had it had taken Britain six months to release details of men charged with attempting to assassinate her uncle Sergei and cousin Yulia in Salisbury?

The two Russians claimed to be weekend tourists, as they explained to RT:

The two men told Simonyan they went to London to *"hang out,"* and decided to also visit Salisbury upon the advice of their friends. The town, situated close to the world-famous Stonehenge, also attracted them because of the Cathedral Church of the Blessed Virgin Mary, *"famous not just in Europe, but in the whole world."*

Asked about the alleged deadly bottle of perfume, they replied: "Don't you think that it's kind of stupid for two straight men to be carrying perfume for ladies? When you go through customs, they check all your belongings. So, if we had anything suspicious, they would definitely have questions. Why would a man have women's perfume in his bag?" Boshirov said.

They also stressed that not only did they not have Novichok in a Nina Ricci bottle, they didn't have it at all, or any other poison for that matter.

Both Petrov and Boshirov sounded distressed as they spoke about how much their lives changed since they were named in the UK as Russian intelligence agents who attempted to assassinate the Skripals. "When your life is turned upside down, you don't really understand what to do and where to go," Boshirov said.[49]

The RT host found the couple to be nervous and perspiring in the studio, so that she had to supply some cognac to 'give them courage.' They did sound rather dopey in the interview, so maybe it was the cognac! They claimed to have some business in the sports and fitness industry but declined to supply details, saying it would compromise their clients. Most people seemed not to believe their story, however they struck me as genuine partly because of their bumbling incoherence in the interview, ie real assassins would have a better story! The intelligence agency 'Bellingcat' tried to claim that these were not their real names and that they worked for Russian intelligence, but I reckon they never showed this.

Scotland Yard was finally able to show CCTV from March 4th, after having been unable to show any for the previous six months: images they released show the two Russians happily pottering around the town in broad daylight. The CCTV shows that they did not catch the first train out of Salisbury after 1 pm or so, but instead they are seen wandering about and doing some shopping; they are *not* seen entering the historic old park, where they supposedly discarded the 'perfume bottle', in a bin.

---

[49] RT 13.9.18 'We're not agents': UK's suspects in Skripal case talk exclusively with RT's editor-in-chief.

Here is a police photo of the two at 1.05 pm walking down Fisherton road, Salisbury. If this is after they have done the deed, then they seem remarkably cheerful and relaxed, as if they were having a good time. That location is just under a mile away from the home of the Skripals and they are walking in a north-Westerly direction towards the home. At 1.08 pm the police photos put them at the junction of Summerlock Approach and Fisherton Street, and we are being told that they have just come from Christie Miller Road where the Skripals live. Or, if you reckon they are just going to the Skripals home (a little behind the narrative schedule) – after all, that is the direction in which they are walking – then they might just have arrived in time to see the Skripals drive off in their car.

The metadata of these famous pictures, of the two Russians in Salisbury, shows that the police prepared them on May 9th, one month before Charlie Rowley allegedly picked the bottle out of the bin: people wondered, how come they waited four months before releasing them to the public?

The two are captured on one CCTV video-sequence walking past a shop window, near to the above location on Fisherton street, going past the Dauwalders Coin and Stamp Shop at 1.49 pm., walking towards the train station. This suggests that they were not going anywhere in a hurry, but were just pottering around. This video belonged to the shop, and is hardly compatible with the police claim that the two had reached the Salisbury train station at 1.51 pm: they could not have been there by then.50

As was mentioned earlier (Chapter 3, page 12), an intelligence source called 'Bellingcat' claimed that the two Russian 'tourists' had three seats booked for the return journey on their plane to Moscow. The suggestion that Mr Skripal wanted to return to Moscow has been confirmed by Vladimir Putin, in an interview with filmmaker Oliver Stone:

> Stone: What has happened to Skripal? Where is he?
>
> Putin: I have no idea. He is a spy, after all. He is always in hiding.
>
> Stone: They say he was going to come back to Russia. He had some information.
>
> Putin: Yes, I have been told that he wants to make a written request to come back.

---

50 'CCTV Footage Shows Petrov & Boshirov Close to the Skripals' The Blogmere 19.9.18: the best website, for local details of the story.

Stone: He knew still and he wanted to come back. He had information that he could give to the world press herein Russia.

Putin: I doubt it. He has broken the ranks already. What kind of information can he possess?[51]

This dialogue seems to imply that Skripal is still alive.

15

White Helmets at Damascus

The Skripal story required a high level of cognitive dissonance in believers, for which reason it (a) had to continually keep developing, with new additions, as distractions, and (b) was punctuated – if that is the expression – by the bombing of Syria, where equally spurious claims about chemical weapons were being applied. In March and April of 2018, *two different packs of British lies* were blossoming in synchrony, causing far-reaching damage: in Douma, Syria and in Salisbury, England.

The expulsion of Russian diplomats caused by the Skripal affair took place just prior to a massive attack upon Damascus on 14th April by US, UK and French airplanes. That event was in turn prior to the scheduled arrival of the

---

[51] http://en.kremlin.ru/events/president/news/61057 'Interview with Oliver Stone,' 19 July 2019

OPCW team in Douma, which was the site of the alleged chemical weapons attack. The OPCW was thereby sidelined, because their visit became fairly meaningless once the whole site had been bombed. It became evident that the UK-founded 'White Helmets' group had set up the phoney CW attack that enabled the bombing: this well-funded group was set up by the British army for such a purpose, whereby it would pretend to be rescuing children from attacks by the Syrian government.

It is remarkable that both Syria and Russia have been demonized, by these psy-ops, British-fabricated mock-events, which ran concurrently. Both stories concerned chemical weapons, and were presumably related to or deriving from the three-week 'Operation Toxic Dagger' rehearsed by the British Army beforehand on Salisbury Plain. Here is a doctor in the Douma hospital commenting on the White-Helmets masquerade:

> Many people burst into the hospital. Among them were those clad in medical outfit but they were not our employees, and I do not think that they were medics at all. They started shouting something about a chemical attack dousing people with water and all this was filmed. As a result, rumours were spread among Douma residents, something which in turn sparked panic … (Dr Jaber, Sputnik news.com, 7th April)

This statement, by a doctor in Syria denying that any CW victims had been treated in his hospital, is analogous to the letter sent by a Salisbury doctor to *The Times* a few weeks earlier, denying that any CW victims had been treated in his hospital. Both cases were responding to a deceptive story woven by British military intelligence. One may see a further analogy, in that the OPCW had in Syria to be marginalised, in order to prevent it from exposing the phoney White Helmets story, while the Syrian government was being blamed for fake CW attack.

Figure: *Veterans Today* image 23.12.18

President Assad in an interview with *The Mail* stated a couple of months after the event, that 'we consider White Helmets to be a PR stunt by the UK.' Likewise, a BBC Syria producer Riam Dalati tweeted that the whole Douma CW story had been fabricated: 'After almost six months investigations, I can prove without a doubt that the Douma hospital scene was staged.'

In response the BBC attempted some damage-control. We quote the insightful Vanessa Beeley from her visit to Syria – interviewed by *Veterans Today* (14.2.19):

So, fundamentally what these mainstream outlets do is put out a narrative which, as I've pointed out, effectively manufactured consent for the unlawful bombing of a sovereign nation, Syria, by the US, France and the UK, post- the Douma alleged attack. But these storylines and these narratives are never retracted; so it remains to be seen whether the BBC will apologise to Syria for having manufactured the consent for the bombing, and whether Riam Dalati and the BBC will apologise to academics and to independent journalists that they smeared at the time for arriving at the same conclusion they've now arrived at.

I've proven and I've written an open investigation based on testimony from civilians in Eastern Ghouta of the White Helmets staging at least one chemical weapon attack one month before Douma… which was actually derailed by the civilians themselves who exposed it on social media etc. The White Helmets have been proven time and time again to be staging events in order to serve the NATO member states' regime change narrative inside Syria. This might start to raise questions over the veracity of the White Helmets reports, bearing in mind that the UK government document has publicly stated that Amnesty International and Human Rights Watch, for example, rely extensively on the evidence of the <u>White Helmets</u> to produce their reports that, again, largely criminalise the Syrian government.

The very fact that France, the UK and the US went ahead and bombed Syria, and as you said it was an extensive bombing operation that targeted alleged chemical weapons manufacturing facilities that were proven afterwards and also reported by OPCW to not be chemical weapons manufacturing facilities, brings into question the legality of that attack. It brings into question the legality of the entire regime change war that has been waged against Syria since 2011, of course instigated by those same nations that bombed after Douma.

But the fact that that the bombing went ahead without any OPCW investigation having been able to take place and based entirely on what is now proven or thought to be spurious information from groups like the White Helmets, that are being funded by the nations that carried out the bombing attack, I mean, this is an extraordinary event; this basically means that the US, the UK and France have completely violated international law time and time again inside Syria and this must be brought into the light, it must be investigated.

That is, alas, unlikely to happen, mainly because Britain has such a servile media. One is touched by Vanessa Beeley's concern for international law but it's doubtful whether UK politicians share her concern in this regard.

The *Pink Floyd's* lead guitarist Roger Walters has denounced the fake gas attack at Douma, asking the powers that bombed Damascus, 'How do you sleep at night?' He described the story set up by the White Helmets as a 'callous and murderous fairytale.' "The White Helmets probably murdered 34 women and children to dress the scene that sorry day in Douma," he posted on his facebook page.

Here is a tweet from US 'Real News' journalist Ben Norton, on how the UK-Government funded 'Integrity Initiative' was pushing the fake 'White Helmets' narrative in Syria.

The story of the bombing of Douma has grown into a thrilling, hyper-realistic 'Call of duty' wargame which has the player as a SAS and/or White Helmet member rescuing babies in Syria from deadly attacks by Russian planes - with Russian soldiers throwing nerve gas about! Not surprisingly, the Pentagon assisted in its creation. Our sanity is here rescued by blogger comments on its website 'Call of Duty: Al Qaeda Atrocity edition.' Eg, here is 'Josh 876': 'The blatant anti-Russian propaganda just confirms that the video game industry is already owned by "The Man" just like the rest of entertainment. And it isn't just geo-political propaganda, it is also the anti-White male stuff (feminism, anti-racism, anti Nationalism and all the usual crap.' Or, Pedro Vaz: 'What's with the Russian genocide happy soldiers? Which war is this supposed to represent/emulate, is it the Soviet Afghan war, because if not then that's one big fictional bullshittery.' Yang Gang: 'Since this game includes Russians in a ME country, "nerve gas" and the White Helmets aka Syria's "moderate" head choppers, presumably players will be able to behead Christians, stage fake gas attacks, rape and enslave Yazidis, and machine gun civilians then dump them into mass graves?' Josh 876[52]

One regrets the poisoning of young minds in this manner.

16

Dead Ducks and the 'Special Relationship'

The whole cost for Salisbury police had been well above ten million pounds. That may seem a lot to pay for one more pack of lies from the British government - but for the holy cause of starting a new cold war against Russia, maybe it was all worthwhile.

---

[52] Charlieintel.com, 'Call of Duty: Modern Warfare Campaign Missions' 30.5.19

A year later, in April of 2019, the New York Times revealed how the newly-appointed Director of the CIA had persuaded Trump to expel the Russian diplomats: she had shown him pictures of kids in hospital plus some dead ducks at the Salisbury pond. Novichok had done this, she asssured him. She, Gina Haspel, had a reputation for the thrill she obtained from seeing people tortured at Guantanamo. She had been appointed to her new position about ten days after the Skripal story appeared, and then towards the end of the month the stories of children at the duckpond seeing the Skripals on or just after noon, broke. Why, they were given bread from the Skripals contaminated with the deadly Novichok that had come straight from the doorhandle – or so the *Mirror, Sun* and *Mail* averred. Have they no shame? America's top torturer thus moved the heart of her President, to endorse what she called the 'strong option' of expelling sixty diplomats.

The *New York Times* article provoked a response from the director of public health at Wiltshire Council, Tracy Daszkiewicz:

> There were no other casualties other than those previously stated. No wildlife were impacted by the incident and no children were exposed to or became ill as a result of either incident.

As well as that categoric denial, Salisbury hospital put out a similar statement, that 'no children were admitted as a result of being exposed to Novichok.' The question here arises as to who is lying, and who gave them false narrative to the CIA, that was used as a basis for the expulsion of Russian diplomats. *The Sun* posted an image of the frightened child and the pond. A local resident realized that this was *the wrong pond*[53]: we're here in the main green area of Salisbury which is the historic Queen Elizabeth gardens,

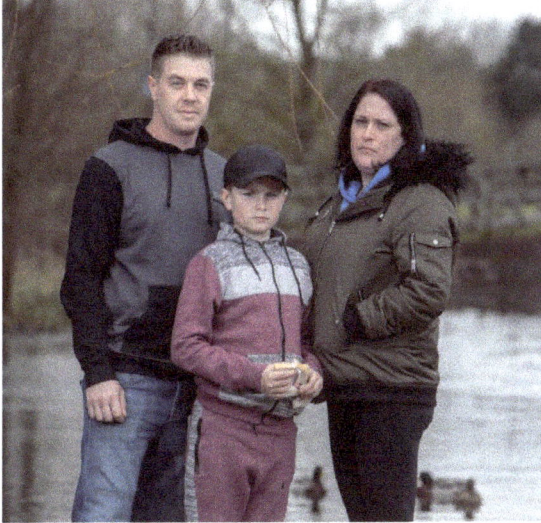

Figure: The Wrong Pond? Twelve-year old Ainan Cooper with parents *The Sun* 28th March

and that is not anywhere near the Maltings, where the Park Bench of Doom was located. One cannot have the Skripals in that park on that day.

Rob Slane spoke to the mother of one of the boys, Mrs Cooper, who recalled how the police had shown her "really clear" CCTV footage of this incident: she there saw Mr Skripal and his daughter (who she said was carrying a red bag). She said she thought that the time on the CCTV showed 1:15pm, but her partner said it was 1:45pm.

---

[53] www.theblogmire.com, 'It's the wrong park!' 10.7.18

The newspaper articles on the young boys who were given bread by the Skripals to feed the ducks appeared over 24-28th of March, with the *Sun* quoting the father Luke as to how they did not suspect anything was wrong until the police turned up two weeks later. His son Aiden is quoted saying that he is scared, too scared to go out, whereas his Father says: "We didn't think anything of it until two weeks later when then the police knocked on our door."[54] No problem was perceived until the police arrived two weeks later and started scaring everyone. The CIA Director gave Trump the dead-ducks-and-poisoned-children story around the 20th-23rd which was immediately before it hit the headlines: probably necessary as those newspapers did carry statements that the medical tests were indicating that no poisoning had been detected.

We apprehend the primary axiom of modern politics, that *the people have to live in fear.*

The Skripal story has been used to ramp up a new cold war against Russia. MI6 plans for the isolation and economic ruin of Russia, including sporting bans and ending cultural exchanges, date from 2015, as revealed by Anonymous. Then early in 2019 facts emerged showing how the UK's 'Institute for Statecraft' Mark Urban had received secret service sponsorship to interview Skripal months before the March 4th incident. For sheer mendacity, which other nation can compare with the UK?

Foreign Secretary Boris Johnson affirmed that: *'British intelligence has a copy of the Russian training manual, which*

---

[54] *The Sun*, 28 March, 'Schoolboy, 12, on how he was exposed to a deadly poison..'

includes instruction on painting nerve agent on doorknobs.'[55] He had seen a copy, he stated; which was however much too secret to show anyone. Did any paper criticize such casual mendacity? On the contrary, he was admired for his ability to grab headlines, and has become the Prime Minister.

As of July 2019, *Russia Today* was fined £200,000 by Ofcom for 'lack of balance' in its programmes. Primarily, this was a result of some well-balanced comments upon the Skripal affair, made by George Galloway on his weekly program 'Sputnik.' The British government's narrative had been "sadly in want of consistency and accuracy" he averred – with which it is hard to disagree. His guest on the program was former Kremlin advisor Alexander Nekrassov, who reckoned that the incident was a "badly prepared provocation": British politicians were "in trouble" he reckoned and so needed a distraction. He was here merely giving expression to a widespread view, that the whole affair had been designed to distract the public from the failing Brexit process.

A month later in August 2019 the US imposed a fresh round of sanctions against Russia, on the basis of the Skripal story, whereby US banks would be prohibited from issuing loans to Russia, and the US would try to stop international banks from doing so.

---

[55] Murray, 'Holes in the Official Skripal Story', 12 July.

17

'Yellow Rain' – how history repeats

Scientists will appreciate the following comment concerning a much earlier episode, featuring alleged use of chemical weapons, drummed up by politicians for their nefarious purposes. It describes a dilemma highly relevant to the Skripal affair:

> The traditions of scientific enquiry, which place the utmost value on peer review and on disclosure of sources and methods, do not sit comfortably into the heirarchical and secretive processes of government.[56]

That is the nub of the matter. If, for example, different bio-labs had been allowed to analyse the content of that 'Novichok' perfume bottle (which surely never existed - however we here suppose that it did, for the sake of argument), and if furthermore they had compared this with samples taken anywhere else, then a conclusion could be reached, which would be a scientific judgement. We would have qualified bio-lab analysts doing what they were professionally trained to do, and a result that was reliable – and the OPCW would at last know what 'Novichok' was. Readers who have come this far will apprehend, why none of that could be allowed to happen! Instead, political actors

---

[56] Julian Perry Robinson, 'Is Yellow Rain Natural?' SIPRI 1984, p.337.

superimposed a narrative, a *pre-determined* narrative, onto what was a mere semblance of scientific enquiry.

The scientific method should involve scientists who do *not* know the answer in advance, who *are* allowed to be sceptical, and who can *disagree* with one another. One much doubts whether these things were the case for the lab workers in Porton Down or the OSCE. Instead, political pressures involving their future careers were applied, and these were shrouded in secrecy.

In 2018 World leaders were meeting together in Mid-March for a G7 summit comprising leaders of Canada, France, Germany, Italy, Japan, the United Kingdom, and the United States, Russia having been excluded. At that meeting on March 15th, the USA came round to accepting the British line concerning the Skripal story. Four of the nations (Germany, France, US and UK) put out a joint statement accusing Russia of having violated the 1925 Chemical Weapons Convention, where nations agreed to ban these dreadful weapons. The four nations brazenly asserted:

> This use of a military-grade nerve agent, of a type developed by Russia, constitutes the first offensive use of a nerve agent in Europe since the Second World War.

A day later I posted this riposte:

> No, you lying snakes, correction:

> This allegation of use of a military-grade nerve agent, is the first such fake-news accusing Russia of using nerve gas since 1982. The British government did indeed make this claim (in 1982, of 'Yellow Rain' in South-East Asia) then it turned out to be a natural substance from bees – the UK

Government never apologized or retracted its untruthful accusation.[57]

Back in 1982, the world was poised for a major United Nations 'Special Session on Disarmament' and there was much hope that it would put a cap on the nuclear arms race. However, the US President Ronald Reagan and the British Prime Minister Margaret Thatcher had a different agenda that involved starting up a new cold war, and so a diversion was needed. This duly arrived in the form of a shocking accusation that the Russians had been using poison gas in various parts of South-East Asia.

On the eve of that US Disarmament session, the 'Hague Report' (Al Hague was the US foreign Secretary) appeared, and it detailed what appeared to be a shocking story. 'Except to the wittingly obtuse, the evidence is conclusive' intoned the Wall Street Journal. The story was obscure, about complaints that had been emanating from Laos and Thailand. The accusation did indeed derail the United Nations disarmament conference, but was it true? The Soviets were shocked and bewildered, at being thus accused. A frightening book *Yellow Rain: A Journey through the terror of Chemical Warfare* appeared in 1982, followed by the more honest *The Yellow Rainmakers* of 1983 by the Australian Grant Evans. One of its last chapters, *Honest Delusion and Evil Propaganda,* should be mandatory reading for any civil servants who believed the Skripal story.

That alleged toxin was indeed – to cut a long story short - bee excrement. 'Yellow rain' was, it turned out, a natural phenomenon.[58] Though tortured logic and the jungles of South-East Asia, accounts of it had ended up in the weighty but delusional *Hague Report*. To its eternal credit, Britain's Porton Down establishment then refused to endorse the American story: it kept noticing that the samples of 'yellow rain' it was sent for analysis contained pollen! No doubt there is a moral here.

Or, maybe just the words of Jesus Christ will suffice: 'It is not what goes into a man's mouth that defiles him, but what comes out of it' (Matthew 15).

....

On March 17th it was announced that Porton Down would be receiving £48 million to develop a brand-new Chemical Warfare Defence Centre; that didn't take long, and illustrates the principle, that those who collaborate in weaving the terror story, are the ones who benefit from it.

Appendix

The US Lyndon Larouche Foundation sent the following petition concerning the effect of the UK propaganda, to President Trump in 2018:

"The Congressional investigations into the origins of the ongoing, fake Russiagate coup against your presidency have revealed that *the Obama Administration used false information and*

---

[58] 'Is Yellow Rain Natural?' by Julian Perry Robinson, *World Armaments and Disarmament SIPRI Yearbook* 1984 pp.377-8, and 'Yellow Rain' SIPRI Yearbook 1985, pp.186-7.

evidence fabricated in London, by official and unofficial British intelligence agents, to justify an unprecedented FBI counterintelligence investigation of your campaign.

Former MI6 agent Christopher Steele told his Department of Justice handler, former Associate Deputy Attorney General Bruce Ohr, that he would "do anything" to prevent Donald Trump's election and was desperate to stop it from happening. Steele was the author of the notorious fake dossier claiming that Donald Trump, having previously been sexually compromised by Vladimir Putin, was working with Putin to defeat Hillary Clinton. Steele's bizarre, amateurish, and totally fake dossier was used by a corrupted FBI to justify steps in its illegal investigation, despite the fact that this dossier was paid for by the Clinton campaign and its facts were unverified.

According to multiple published reports, Obama's CIA Director, John Brennan, convened an illegal intelligence task force at the CIA to launder and investigate fake dirt on Trump, produced by a British spy circle led by former MI6 chief Sir Richard Dearlove for purposes of destroying the Trump presidential campaign. Brennan did this because, he said, Donald Trump's election would jeopardize the "special relationship" between U.S. and British intelligence agencies. Dearlove had played a key role in the faked intelligence which led the United States into the Iraq War.

LaRouchePAC, through a previous petition to President Trump on August 10, 2017 — and to Congress on December 29, 2017 — called for complete exposure of the British attempt to nullify the 2016 U.S. election based on British strategic interests. At the time, virtually no one else thought the British were the source of foreign interference in the 2016 elections. That fact is now widely recognized. The so-called "resistance," both within and without the government, is stalling further release of key documents to Congressional committees in order to win the midterm elections and begin impeachment proceedings in the House of Representatives.

The British are conducting an international campaign to smear and militarily and economically confront Russia and China because the City of London financial and imperial order is economically and morally bankrupt and has no plan to build a future for humanity over the course of the next 50 years. This British campaign is not in the interest of the United States, and, Mr. President, you were elected in substantial part on the promise to end America's useless wars on behalf of British strategic objectives.

The complete exposure of the British/Obama Administration subversion of the Trump presidency represents a unique opportunity for Americans to take our country back: to, once again, fully embrace the profound difference between the British imperial system and the American system of political economy created by Alexander Hamilton and advanced by Lyndon LaRouche. The British system produces the degradation of the majority of the population for the wealth of the few; the American system produces general prosperity."

The Larouche Foundation commented on the story[59]:

"The liberated documents show that Sir Andrew Wood and Pablo Miller, Sergei Skripal's MI6 handler, who are both players in Christopher Steele's *Orbis Business Intelligence,* also have significant relationships to the Initiative. Skripal and his daughter were poisoned in Salisbury, England, in one of 2018's more infamous intelligence hoaxes targeting Russia. Steele, of

---

[59] larouchepac.com 'President Trump: Declassify All Documents & Information Concerning British Subversion Of Your Campaign;' also Larouche, 'Russiagate Is Being Transformed into an Exposure of the British Coup,' Jan 2019.

course, wrote the very dirty and obviously fake dossier on Donald Trump and Vladimir Putin which has sustained the Russiagate scandal for almost two years in the United States, throwing this country into a McCarthyite hysteria…"

At the center of the Institute's very military operations, is the use of propaganda directed simultaneously at both the government and the general population. Institute personnel lobby governments on behalf of war-party policies against Russia and China, for example, in their disguise as private parties, while the Institute itself is being paid, as a think-tank, by the very same governments. At the same time, the Institute's media contacts echo the entirely concocted government "debate" to the general population. This circular churning of the media sphere is what Obama's former security advisor Ben Rhodes called creating a public opinion "echo chamber." Rhodes cut his national security chops by helping with production of the fraud known as the 9/11 Commission Report. This methodology, fully implemented in the British propaganda and regime change operation against Putin, which began with the Litvinenko poisoning in 2006 and dramatically escalated in 2014, has created an astounding and deranged war fever against Putin in Britain and throughout Europe."

'An idiot's guide to the Skripal affair'
by *Panopticon*, at The Syrian Observatory for Human Wrongs,
here reproduced with kind permission

A sad, funny story of Sergei and Yulia –
not 'funny ha-ha', but funny peculiar…
One Sunday in March they decided to eat
at a nice little café, then stopped at a seat

where they both felt unwell at the very same minute –
now I think that's quite a coincidence, 'innit?
So an ambulance came for the pair, as requested.
But when they were studied, and prodded, and tested,
nefarious substances in them were found –
and not only there, but spread all around
old Salisbury town, up hill and down valley –
(the High Street is now known as 'Chemical Alley').
A passing D.S. who just happened to be there,
was poisoned like them when he went off to see where
they lived – or did he succumb at the scene?
(His bosses told two different stories on screen).
And while a good nurse who had tended them well
suffered no side effects, 'far as I can tell,
some thirty-eight people were treated as victims,
but I think that someone was taking the mick, since
a day or two after those numbers were stated
the whole bloody lot of them evaporated.
*** Hmm. ***
The media descended like swivel-eyed dervishes,
paid no attention to church Sunday services;
campanologists' melodies had to be quietened,
so BBC viewers could all be enlightened:
"Could you silence those chimes, my parochial friend?"
"Well I could, but at least can we hear the bell end?"
Now Boris mistakenly took that as cue
to appear on the telly, and give us his view
that the case had been cracked by his government sources,
e'en though the police had advised "Hold your horses";
his bods back at Whitehall had worked round the clock
to identify something called 'Doorknobichok' TM
which he claimed had been smeared on the victims' front
door,

under cover of darkness on March 3 or 4.
'Twas a devilish stuff that will kill you in seconds,
and was put there by Russkies (or so his boss reckons).
So lethal that only a tenth of a gram
would transport you to heaven, to visit your gran.
"So we have two deceased?" the reporters surmised;
"No, they're not dead" said Boris, "just hoskripalised!".
*** I thank you. ***
Then someone observed something really quite odd –
that the door didn't seem to have bothered the plod
who was tasked with the duty of guarding the place,
long before it was clear that a poison was traced.
"So how could this be?" it was asked of the Tory,
who conferred with his bosses, and then changed his story:
"No, it wasn't the handle, but gas-tainted air
in the Skripals' jalopy, 'cause Vlad put it there!"
Then when this didn't wash, he tried yet another –
"it was smuggled from Moscow by Yulia's mother! (in
law)"
In one last attempt to convince us that Putin
had ordered his henchmen to go put the boot in:
"They may have consumed it at breakfast, you see –
in Ricincles or Special K(GB);
for although it would seem like the plot of a thriller,
I'm convinced that our Vlad is a cereal killer!"
*** Hmmm. ***
Then a cordon was thrown around Salisbury town,
which was only a bus ride from old Porton Down
(a village connected to our alleged traitor –
for Sergei is he – but more of that later).
The government said that their duty of care,
because of the obvious dangers in there
meant they might have to pull down the café and pub,

so the locals would have to go elsewhere for grub;
And because of the contaminated front door,
their dwelling might need to be razed to the floor.
Well, this understandably raised some concerns
with the Salisbury folk, who took it in turns
to request some advice, because nobody knows
if they'd gotten the stuff on their shoes, or their clothes:
"Should we burn our belongings, or dump them at sea?"
"Nah, just wash 'em on 'quick rinse' at forty degrees".
"And what of that sinister place up the lane
where your poisons are made, is that whence it came?"
"If you don't mind me saying, your question's absurd,
as of Doorknobichok TMay, we never have heard,
except for the stockpiles we keep for ourselves,
and they are all safe and secure on our shelves".
***   Oops.   ***
The blame was laid squarely on Moscow and Vlad
(as we know from our Bond films that Russians are bad);
expulsion of diplomats worldwide arranged;
accusations thrown, and insults exchanged.
All cultural visits were cancelled or put off,
and Julie Assange had his internet cut off.
Then lo! and behold, our story got murky,
in a village you'll find in a country near Turkey.
The Syrian leader, one Bashar Assad,
was repelling invaders, which made the West mad;
but just as his victory was nearing at last,
his own population he cruelly gassed –
or so we were told by the Powers That Be,
who strung us a line, didn't want us to see
that some brave independents were taking a risk,
like Bartlett and Beeley, Stuart and Fisk,
to show us the true situation in Douma –

if the press did its job we'd have realised sooner
that far from Assad being a monster, and hated
by all of his people, he was celebrated
and trusted to stand up as their only true hope,
in the face of attacks from the U.S. and Europe.
And he wasn't a 'butcher', on murderous mission,
but a family man, and a licenced optician.
***   We should've gone to Specsavers.   ***
Emotional images filled up our screens,
showing suffering women, and babies, and teens;
they were choking on chlorine, which made us all furious –
but no men affected, which did seem quite curious…
The West didn't wait, we accepted the claim
that the evil Assad was entirely to blame.
He was guilty of war crimes, as evidence proved –
for the good of the people, he must be removed!
Notwithstanding the signs that the Syrians may seem
broadly in favour of Mr. A's 'regime'
and the fact that with Russia they had some protection
from outside attacks, or their own insurrection.
Our Washington friends would insist that they need some
of Uncle Sam's good ol' American freedom
which had been so successful, I'm frequently told,
where nations had hardships, and oil, gas, and gold.
The narrative blaming Assad for the crimes
was reported as fact in The Sun and The Times
and most western leaders were keen to appease the
hawkish intentions of Boris and Theresa.
But a doubt did remain that the entire event
might have been a 'false flag', with malicious intent –
would our lovable 'BoJo' condone such a stunt?
Yes he would, because he's an untrustworthy cad….
****

Before we continue I think that we ought'ta
return to the poor stricken father and daughter
whose problems all started when they were infected
with poison – but how this event was connected
to wider concerns internationally,
and the threat of an outbreak of World War III
can be found in the c.v. of old Mister S.,
and the time he was caught and was made to confess
that a Brit double-agent was his part-time job,
with some colleagues betrayed for a few extra bob.
So a jail cell in Moscow was where he would stay,
till a spy swap arrangement took him to U.K.
Here he stayed for a while, but he yearned to go home,
which worried the spooks listening in on his phone.
Was this why the homesick old Russian was nobbled?
Or was it the claim that with help he had cobbled
together a dossier aimed at the POTUS,
that the Democrats hoped would dissuade U.S. voters
And result in the triumph of Hillary Clinton,
with subsequent guaranteed hell, fire and brimstone?
The plot didn't work, and old Trump was elected,
but whatever the reason the pair were infected,
our government said "It's clear if you ask us,
that this can be traced all the way to Damascus,
for it shows that the Russians will use any measure
to help young Assad and incur our displeasure;
The agents of Putin can poison to order
And will have no respect for law, life or border.
But nothing must stop the success of our plan
which began in Baghdad and will end in Tehran."
***   "Highly Likely"   ***
So despite all the evidence proving this crisis
was carefully staged by the West's friends in ISIS,

these facts were ignored by the Beeb and the papers,
who called for an end to the Syrian's capers.
This gave our P.M. all the reasons she needed
to mount an attack, with all protests unheeded,
along with her chums in the U.S. and France,
but they thoughtfully notified Vlad in advance;
for this wasn't a true act of war, but a sham,
to convince all the voters that they had a plan.
A fortune was spent on some shiny new rockets
(replacements would benefit shareholders' pockets);
so where shall we fire 'em? Mrs. May scratched her head:
"Well we wouldn't want anyone injured, or dead,
but we know where he hides his consignment of gases,
to terrorise all of his downtrodden masses,
so we'll send in these missiles, with shock and with awe,
and we'll blow the dumps up, which will shorten the war".
"Won't those missiles release all the toxins therein,
to kill one and all – a terrible sin??"
A blank look appeared, then Theresa retorted:
"I'd not thought of that, could you please not report it?"
***   Jesus H. Christ.   ***
The bombing commenced, on irrelevant target
So the Maybot could emulate her idol, Margaret,
and show that in conflict she was strong and mighty
but meanwhile, something was stirring in Blighty…..
Our young Russian lady, whose certain demise
was expected, suddenly opened her eyes
just as Easter approached, in her hospital prison,
To be greeted with cries of "Christ, she is risen!"
And to make matters worse, she had borrowed a phone
and confirmed her good health to her cousin back home –
which scuppered the prospect that Yulia could
have been quietly forgotten, or silenced for good.

But what of her daddy, who'd been at death's door
'cause he'd got on the outside of A-234?
Well I'm glad to report that, despite the prognosis
that follows ingestion of such fatal doses
both he and the bobby awoke from their comas,
which filled sceptics' nostrils with fishy aromas;
for what kind of poison, designed to be lethal
has no such effect on these three lucky people?
There were so many questions we needed to ask,
but journalists didn't seem up to the task;
this global concern that had Doomsday advancing
took a sad second place behind 'Strictly Come Dancing'.
And the government proved they had something to hide
by imposing a ban on reporting worldwide.
***   Russians can dance too!   ***
So the Skripals survived , but we still couldn't see them,
the Powers That Be had denied them their freedom
And took them away to location unknown
without access to newspapers, TV or phone.
(I thought that their chances were now slim-to-none –
remember the plotline of 'Capricorn One'?)
Then just as our hopes had been starting to fade
our Yulie appeared in a green English glade
and read out a statement, author unknown,
that asked if we kindly would leave her alone;
for although she was well she would like to appeal
that we give her more time to get through her ordeal;
and this sentiment really had nothing to do
with the fact that her kidnappers bloody well knew
that if they could escape from their new adversaries
they'd scoot back to Moscow and sing like canaries.
For if you think that Russia was guilty, I'll tell you
where we can meet up, there's a bridge I can sell you…

****

Epilogue

So that was the last that we saw of the pair
but it isn't the end of this sorry affair
For although we're not sure why the Skripals were picked
on
It's clear the official response was pure fiction
and twisted to play to the NeoCons' plan
to annihilate Syria, to get to Iran
and to demonise Russia, who stands in the way
of a world dominated by U.S. of A.
Who'd support this assault? The U.K. and E.U. did
and lied through their teeth, 'cause they think we're
all stupid.
But the crimes we commit on behalf of our rotten
regimes to our neighbours, will not be forgotten;
their patience will only protect us so far
then the West will provoke an unwinnable war.
And we'll wonder how things could have got to the state
where we fear for ourselves and our own children's fate
but forget that this land, where democracy lives
is now governed by liars, and traitors, and spivs
who will rig the roulette wheel for guaranteed wins
till we find that they've played us like cheap violins;
whose fake manifestos fight for our attention
with lies about justice, and healthcare, and pensions;
who'll cheat, kill and steal, till they've conquered all
nations
preaching hatred of Africans, Russians and Asians
and throughout their pursuits they'll accept no dissent
and it's all on behalf of the great one per cent.
And we'll ask God how He could allow such a sin
And He'll say "It was you lot who voted them in".

INDEX